SUNSHYN LOVE

SECURE IN HER THOUGHTS

RASCHON KING

Sunshyn Love

© 2015 Raschon King

ISBN-13: 978-0692465424

ISBN-10: 0692465421

Published by Broken Bars Publishing

www.brokenbarspublishing.com

Printed in the United States of America

Dedication

I'm writing a different kind of book because I'm a different kind of person!!! My thanks to God for giving me the gift to write. Without Him there would be no book. To all of my supportive family members, without you pushing me there would be no completion of two books!!!

Thanks to my mother, Glenda Rita London, who had master skills at writing five page letters. I chose to go in her footsteps as she has gone on to Heaven. My sisters, Angela Gavin and Latisha Yearby, have been my best cheerleaders, cheering me on from the very beginning when I was writing plays and short writings back in the day. When it came down to it, Angela Gavin stepped up beyond the clouds of joy encouraging me, saying, "Girl you did your thing and I am grateful for all your skills and then some."

To my brother, Robert Gavin, thanks for lending me your wife; she never put you before my book. To my dearest friend, Dewayne, I started writing again when I met you. A vision was created and you pushed me to go on. You were my first prime reader. You always said my poems were the best. Thank You!

To my friend, Mr. Howard, you read just one of my writings ("Puzzled") and when you were done you looked at me and said, is this about me? You suggested that I write a book. You also said my writing was unique, and I totally agreed. Thank You!

To my kids, nieces, nephews and cousins, thanks for the support in bringing "Wishing, Wishing Well" to life. You performed it at church in the Black History Program thanks to Angela Gavin!!!

To Guy Fluellen, my unlegal consultant, you gave me advice on how not to share my writings without them first being published. Sadly my first one is in your obituary. R.I.P. my friend.

Last but not least, my counselor Dr. Brown. Thanks for the motivation. Your powerful words of wisdom got me to the finish line. Thank You!

Table of Contents

<u>Wishing, Wishing Well</u>

Wishing wishing well, wishing wishing well
I'm going to drop your name in the wishing well
I'm going to sound the bell
I'm going to lift my head
I'm going to stomp my feet
As praises goes up
Blessings come down
Wishing wishing well, wishing wishing well
I been thinking of you
I been dreaming of you
My spirit tells me
Something's not right
Wishing wishing well-wishing wishing well
Did-did you know
Jesus dies for me-Jesus died for you
If you don't know-now you know
As praises go up blessings come down
I'm going to drop your name in the wishing well
I'm going to sound the bell
I'm going lift my head
I'm going to stomp my feet
As praises go up, blessings come down
Wishing wishing well-wishing wishing well
As blessings come down
Our family will smile
Trusting in Jesus
Makes our world go round
Loving Jesus
Makes our world go round
Wishing wishing well-wishing wishing well
Hey
As every knee shall bend
Every head shall bow
Every eye shall close
Every tongue confess

Sunshyn Love

As praises go up, blessings come down
As praises go up, blessings come down
Wishing wishing well, wishing wishing well
I'm going to drop your name in the wishing well
I'm going to sound the bell
I'm going to lift my head
I'm going to stomp my feet
As praises go up, blessings come down
Wishing, wishing well-wishing, wishing well

<u>With Every</u>

Old leaf there's a new one
Falling off a tree startling a battle ground
Old leaves you hear them crunching
When you're walking on them
Sounds like they're talking to you
With no explanation as you walk your guided path
New ones laying on the grass and sidewalks
Just like life greets you head on
How do you do and you say
I've fallen and I can't even get back up
Wisdom speaks you're stronger than you think
The wind begins to blow leaves all around you
Looking like an army of men coming for you
Have faith rise and shine
A battle with no ground is like waking up next to
nothing
Refusing to live and stumbling across a rock when
you need a brick and
Your shine outshines your shine
Wait you're looking in the mirror priceless moments
You and you against the world pick up a leaf and
while you're at it
Pick up patience pray and let God solve your
problems
Never fail at succeeding when God has your back
Be a witness and testify to your greatness
Of how you turned over a new leaf in your life!!!

<u>Brown Queen</u>

The woman of our dreams you're simply amazing
Raising everybody just right yes you fussed
You just wanted us to get things right
You kept us in check
When you thought we were doing wrong
You seen clear through us
Often calling us by our whole name
Which often meant take a seat and wonder why
you're here
You taught life lessons in your own way
You always said never have a one-track mind
Do what I tell you and you won't go wrong
Advice we definitely needed
Brown Queen our human spirit knew what soul food
was all about
Sunday dinner always on time
Ham, mac n cheese, sweet potatoes, greens
Just to name a few of the dishes being cooked up and
Yes we were ready to eat until the last drop was gone
Wash your hands and kids first is what she always said
Brown Queen Caught You By The Heart
Always always had handy advice to give out
She had been there exactly where you were once
Just in a different time frame so
She was more like a teacher with all her soulful
experience!!!

Mirror Mirror

On the wall who's the most
Handsome of them all Is it Is it Is it him
The one that dances on a tree
Noooooooooo ok didn't think so
It's not that many mirror mirror
Is it the one who plays hide n seek
Through the mountains and woods
Hmmmmmm I don't think so
Ok now pay attention is it the one
Who looks good in everything
Even a jacket and a coat well is it is it could be
The only thing is your heart will tell you
Even on a rainy day his smile got you
All dang mirror I just wanna know
Who got eyes for me easy you dooooooooooo
Ok silly mirror how about ask me
Nahhhh you won't tell ok let me ask you mirror
If my heart knows will his heart know too
Possibility on a good day
Silly mirror scams are for walls
Just one more question mirror mirror
Do you think I'll ever win his heart bet on it! Done!

<u>Never Mind Me</u>

I'm just a writer
Trying to get my writing skills in
The more I write
The more I release
The more I think
The more I let go
The better I feel
Never mind me simply because
The more I give of self the less tired I feel
The heavier side of me is now much lighter
That weight I no longer have to carry upon me
A gift of knowledge fills vacancies
That now exist you didn't see this before
The treasure I hold within me is golden and
Very very dear to my representation of my life
I must live it until my end of time
Higher standards strong foundation solid grounds
I'm making my way you see those struggling
footprints
It wasn't easy getting to this point but I'm here now
and
There's no turning back no shame in a serious game
Just a humble she, her and me understanding the
values of life
Never put someone down unless later on
You want them to come back and step all over you
while they're rising to the top.

<u>Royal Blue</u>

Reason why
I chose
Royal Blue
I found a loyalty
In you
No matter what
You simply had my back
You gave your all
Even when you had nothing
To give except advice
Free of charge
You often said
Keep writing
Don't stop until your heart
Says you're done
I agreed
I'm still writing
Don't look like I'm ever gonna be done
So much to be said
So many thoughts
God has blessed me with this skill
Of writing how I feel and
I think I do it well
From being
Puzzled, Digging Deep, Creative Woman
Brown Queen, When My Best Depended On You
Wishing Well and Phenomenal Man
Just to name a few
I've done my best
To creatively write
My own fashioned way
I like it
Wishing you do too
Sending my best
When there only was a few

But
Word got out and
Now there's so many of you
Supporting my efforts of being number one
To my best book and the reviews priceless
Hmmm my mother and Guy
Would be oh so happy for me and the fabulous book
Thanks everyone for everything
I've done me proud and
To the chick who said I wouldn't do anything with
my life
Baby
Look at me now just keep looking cause there's more
to come!!!

<u>I Want To Be Pretty</u>

With you
A gift God gave to me
The day I was born
I now want
To share it with you
Letting my presence adorn you
As my hopes and dreams
Enlighten you
I stand
A beautiful natural woman
Never casting a stone but
Every time I'm with you
One turns over a new lease
On my life
When you're near
My pretty shines
A bit more than normal
I'm drowning in love and
It feels so good to be saved by you
A comfort zone of exoticness
A treasure of a gift
Blessed by a treasure of a heart of purity
I'm beautiful naturally but my shine is with you!!!

<u>Rain Drops</u>

Loosely on my head
Feeling like my storm
Is coming to an end
Mountains of hope
Soaking in my skin
A rainbow
So high up in the sky
Feeling lucky
Feeling free
Feeling lucky
Feeling free
Can't be nobody but me
Stars twinkling in the skies
An hour of darkness
A minute of no time
Standing still
A second of uplifting
Somebody else's dream
You got it
If only for a day
Flowers while you're living
Dinner while you're breathing
A smile simply because
You're irresistible and
Caring is sharing
Giving the gift of you
Free and dear
To the heart
Pray daily
Lift up your hands
Give thanks
While you're here!!!

Raschon King

<u>Curtain Call</u>

Chairs
All around me
I'm dancing
In my seat
Music is playing
It's my favorite jam
Can't wait to get up
I'll be
Standing on my feet
Screaming
It's my time
To shine
Rise Shon Rise
Say
What you mean
And
Mean what you
Say
Don't hold back now
It's
Curtain Call
Time
People didn't believe
You had your own mind
They judged you
Before
It was your time
Rise Shon Rise
Look all around you
All the smiling faces
Someone
Adores you
Someone
Even loves you
Giving thanks to Jesus

11

Sunshyn Love

When everyone
Has failed me
He's my best friend
He's my everlasting rock
Watch out
You see
The spotlight shining
Looking for my body
Awww
It's my time to shine
Taking steps
To make it
Up
On the stage
People
All around me
Haters
Even stare
Thought
I couldn't do it
Fooled you
Curtain Call
Is for everybody
Who
Has a dream
Rise Shon Rise
If you
Believe in yourself
With
No hesitating
Only
Smart demonstrating
You can do it
Yes you truly can
Curtain Call

If For Once Things Would Go My Way

If For Once I wouldn't have to live
In a fantasy world If For Once
I wouldn't have to pretend
To do what I've always wanted to do
My life would be great and things
I enjoy wouldn't have to be swept
Under the carpet to wait
For the right day or time
If For Once a dream would come true
Without me sleeping through the night
A miracle wouldn't take years to lift up
A soulful mind a touch wouldn't hurt and
A vision I would be able to see with my
Two naked eyes
As the strength in me would receive
A beautiful power that overturns every wrong
That wanted to be right and if
Love wasn't the focus just a silent cure
For the body to feel when nothing else mattered
Got a lot of growing to do life changes daily and
Nothing stays the same my remedy
Get a glass of power and get stronger as you gain
strength
Move forward and leave your weaknesses behind!!!

<u>Milestones</u>

Inside of bridges little steps
Under the overpass
Visions of the unseen
Awake you are except you feel asleep
No one seems to see you
Invisible you are
As a calm settles over you
The power of the mayhem
Busting out the seams
Visibility captures much
The mind goes into difficult mode
Thoughts of the arisen
You seem to be thinking out loud
No one hears you except their staring
You're not the center of attention
Just a basic statue when the fog clears
Everyone walks away you're on your own
Just like floating on an ocean
Drowning in a mission of being noticed
Except no one sees you
It's a lonely world when you surround yourself
With a bunch of hope
The lights around you are dim!!!

<u>Snapshot</u>

Daily visions of superior moments in life
Stepping up looking back
Yesterday, today and tomorrow all different
The album of life got you displaying many roles
Smile life's special moments got you moving forward
Missions being accomplished that's sentimental value
Journeys no longer sinking in the undercover sand
Walking the walk of controlling a destiny of faith
Thousand dollar random chick
No clothes just a naked soul
Snapshot somebody wants that picture
Emptiness is her feeling
Her spirit incomplete
She knows what not to do
So she keeps on walking
No one is rooting for her failure is the plan
Not one person stopped her as her feet kept walking
Focused only she knew her plan
Folks whispered and watched and waited
Just to see her and she finally waved her hand and
spoke
No one knows where I've been oh my road has been
rocky
Truth to the matter is I'm on my way up so please
Stop looking down on me don't need no crowd I
simply got me!!!

<u>Love Got Me Busy</u>

Thinking of you
How true to my soul
Every breath
Every desire
Every want
Every need
Your face
Your body
Your lips
Kisses my thoughts
Your journey
I'll travel the roads with you
Your mind got me
The stars
Got me wishing for you
As I lay in bed at night
As my toes twinkle
Longing for your touch
Love got me busy
Waiting
Relaxing and willing
To give my all!!!

<u>Magical</u>

When sadness fills your soul
Thank God
Change is coming
A smile creeps on your face
As you're sitting there thinking
About all the things
You have overcome
The dark wall that was once put up
Has been destroyed by a happiness
You can't explain
A joy sparkles in your eyes
The pain that once took over your body
No longer resides cause
You have learned to let it go
You're no longer carrying extra baggage
That used to weigh you down
The load is light
The cloudiness that used to fill your head
Has evaporated
The calmness has melted the storm
Now you're feeling great and looking good
I even see a smile
A magical effect of loving yourself!!!

<u>Peaceful Thinking</u>

Mountain so high
Refused to climb it
Fear kicked in
Roughing up thoughts
Moments like this
Takes the go-getter by surprise
Reaching the top seems endless
Once a dream
Now reality
Focus
Don't give up
If you think you can
You can
Believe and receive
Undo the undone
Don't stress about it
Be about it
Cheers
To the man and woman
That takes a stand
Even when standards aren't met
Keep trying
Always
Be doubt-free
Don't stop living
Life waits for no one
Days won't wait until you're ready
To begin again
The clock keeps ticking
Ready or not hit or miss
Perfect or not
Don't stop trying
When you think your right is wrong
Challenge yourself
To make good faithful changes

Sometimes you got to experience
The good, bad and ugly
To stay focused
Remember a quitter
Never wins
So stay on track and
Run your race
Until you get to the finish line
Motivate yourself and enjoy
Positive feedback from
Your mind that encourages your all
Peaceful thinking is good for your mind!!!

<u>Push Me Forward</u>

No time for
Turning back these hands of time
No time for thinking
Of the could've, would've, should've
Placing my feet where they need to be
At the right moment right now
Mistakes were made excuses were a challenge
Picking up the pieces of a wounded journey
Changes described as
Take me as I am I'm only human
I have fallen not afraid to say I got back up and there
were times
When curveballs were coming at me so strong and
fast
I stumbled and ducked and then
I put my hands up and said Lord I surrender I give
you my all
I am who I am
Peace in my heart, strength in my bones
Don't let me lean
Lord You Are My Rock
Pain and suffering I no longer claim Lord I give my
all to you
Anyone who wants to walk in my shoes
Will notice they won't fit; what's for me is for me
Push Me Forward
No reruns no returns, love yourself you can't go
wrong!!!

<u>L O V E</u>

Through the peaceful skies
A powerful mold
As stars forming in the darkened hours
L O V E
Filling your body
Two souls no longer undercover
Spirits floating above the horizon
Embracing the stretch in the miles
That distance you from me
L O V E
A shared source the eyes focused
On a love so rare
You love me but you don't tell
The heart always knows
What the lips don't speak
The details of how you're feeling
Explodes on my plate
A body so happy to accept
What you been through
No matter the mistakes
Your love
As only I can absorb this soaking
Your sweat and all your tears
I'll gladly wipe away with my magical touch I got you!

<u>Spaces</u>

Deep down inside me
Breaking down the barriers
Of the walls that surround me
A come out to a get out
Spaces deep down inside me
Covered with my thoughts
Of only loving
A one-in-a-trillion you
Spaces deep down inside me
Twisting my words
As long term sentences
Turn into silent vibes
Of touching you
Spaces deep down inside me
Got me wanting to know so much
More about you
Thoughts filling my mind
Of how needing you appeals to me
You're a satisfying happiness
That comforts my heart
Spaces deep down inside me
Love you for who you are
Visions seen from the pure naked eye!

<u>Tried and Convicted</u>

Torn to pieces
Evidence
Somebody else's voice
The splitting of family and friends
New to this
Admitting you did one wrong
Is a testimony
To someone else's test
Closed doors you wasn't looking in but
Judged one by what you heard
Not by what you know or seen
Guilty of being a star witness
To something you know about
A face may be happy on the outside except
The body language describes something totally
different
No one paying attention to the inside blues
Facial expressions speak for themselves
Leaving the mouth dry and nerves on edge
No spoken words to search a soul that all others have
declared war
On the outside just feelings falling off like leaves from
a tree
The supporting fears climbing up your difficult
mountain
Own up to releasing and letting go
No greater power than being a better you
No greater struggle than surviving what you been
through!

<u>Breaking Down the Barriers</u>

Breaking down the barriers of
The walls that surround you
A come out to a get out
A rise to a beautiful shine
A vision to a powerful reality
A hole dug but yet you're left standing tall
A testimony dedicated to your own life
As well as shared with others
You picked the lock
To a great release of what others denied you
Doors that were once closed have opened
With brand new opportunities
Dual moments now sit at your fingertips
Chasing dreams that you once slept on
The rainbow you only seen from afar
Is now footsteps away hands down
As you know you can do what needs to be done
Challenge yourself and moves will be made
Take your time and give plenty of effort
Life only gets better from here
Know that downs only stay down if you refuse to go
up
Sometimes you got to change your game plans
Reinvent yourself make your wrongs right and
continue forward...

<u>Puzzled</u>

Her look told it all
She couldn't hide the sadness
That appeared upon her face
So many
People just didn't understand her
The reason being she was special
She was nice and kind
She never let negativity fill her thoughts
Puzzled
Simple things never got in her way
She loved being her
The way she combed her hair
The clothes she wore
The way she walked without stumbling, confidence
The way she talked with pride, positivity
The way she smiled, happiness
Puzzled
She believed in herself
She did what was best for her
She set goals and challenged herself often
Her life was a marathon her plan was to succeed
above and beyond
Puzzled
When problems arrived in her life
She got down on her knees and prayed to God
Her faith is what kept her
She realized being humble was not just a good thing
but also a great thing
Puzzled
She realized she didn't need to follow in anyone else's
footsteps
When she could be her own leader
She was blessed in so many talented ways
A mind is a terrible thing to waste
Smile

It's Your Birthday Right, Angela Gavin

You have the right to do whatever your heart desires
It's your day
You have the right not to forget to take your
medicine
It's your day
You have the right to eat a big healthy breakfast
You have the right to eat a big piece of sugar-free
cake
It's your day
You have the right to put one candle on your cake
cause your breath is too short to blow out all 50
It's your day
You have the right to relax, chill, stay in bed as long
as you like
It's your day
You have the right to smile cause not everyone made
it over the hill
You have the right not to keep silent, scream as loud
as you want
You have the right to take a bow, as everyone who
loves and cares for you will call, text you saying happy
birthday girl! Because you're you
It's your day, Angie

February I'm Famous

February is the month for celebrating black
Americans of all kinds
Famous non-famous if you accomplished something
Thank God you did that no hesitation no
demonstration
So let's go starting with me ending with you
Who Am I
I am black I represent black history not just in
February but every month
I love the color of my skin it represents who I came
from
I'm not famous just talented and bright I enjoy
writing and it's a gift
From my mother just to let you know
I reside in Detroit born and raised and I am the first
writer of my book
It's not duplicated or imitated just my creative style
writing
Who Am I: Raschon King With Positive Notes
Know that you got the power to do anything and
everything
You put your mind to I never thought I would be a
writer
But here I am exclusively unique
I started writing at 17 and still going strong matter of
fact
I began writing plays for church first
Noah's Ark, Christmas Star and Rosa Parks I'm Not
Getting Up
I enjoyed writing then and I really enjoy it now
I had time to expand and explore my mind
I celebrate being a black female writer in my own
rights
Because I'm black, talented and nothing I write is
owned by someone else

Sunshyn Love

In order to do anything you just got to keep your
focus and go for it!!!

<u>Sunshine Surprises My Story</u>

One day I was at home the day was peaceful
The sun was shining what a beautiful beginning
Of a fabulous day as I was doing my normal activities
There was a knock on the door I said hmmmmm
I wonder who that could be I looked out the
peephole
It was the mailman I said who is it
In my surprised voice he said in a deep voice mailman
miss
He said in a deep voice mailman miss I opened the
door and
Said yes he said I have a special delivery I said really I
don't want it
He said can't return it I said leave it on the porch
Now the day was sunny but it was a little cool I said
Where are your pants he said I'm a stripper baby
I got all your mail and I said I hope one of those
packages
Got a check inside or no dollars for you
Plus it's beautiful outside no way I'm making it rain or
snow lol
He said miss I'm here to do a job I said I'm not hiring
he said look miss
I said can't see I'm not wearing my glasses he said
Do you want me to dance for you or what I said go
ahead never had a porch dance
He looked at me and said miss I'm done I said I'm
sure you are wit your cute self
He was blushing I said can you twerk he said of
course I can I said well let me see you
Twerk your booty off my porch and watch where
you're going no insurance if you fall
You get the stairs and asphalt you land on he said
dang straight up I said right on big pimping
He said you so crazy I said you so right he said so
long I said see you later mailman surprise!!!

<u>Passing Out Poetry</u>

I took my time
Wrote everything right
Did my acknowledgments
If I forgot to mention you
It wasn't on purpose
Please don't blame my heart
If you pre-read my work and
Didn't judge me I appreciate you
Sometimes I had to do a power exchange
With Raschon turning into Shonie
She had a lot to say but
You be the judge because
Me and her one of the same
Raschon always in her feelings and
Well Shonie out of the ordinary
Pain hit me hard this year lost a
Very good friend and this book
Dedicated to him Guy Fluellen
Moving right along
Sometimes you got to hide it to keep going strong
I wrote about it because I needed to feel peace
Within me don't judge me I'm human enough said!!!

Raschon King

<u>Silence Covers My Mouth</u>

As I listen
Guy, after hearing your voice
On my voicemail April 22, 2014
All I wanted to do was sleep
My eyes got so tired
My heart torn to pieces
A part of me gone
Got me feeling weak
Tears rush my face but I simply
Try to hold them back
I'm breaking indeed
Feeling like I'm done
My inside voice says Shon
I told you not to listen but you just couldn't resist
I know he was your friend and life without him
You never imagined gosh I know it hurts
Earth objects beautiful flowers and trees
I can't find peace within me to settle this battle of you
being gone
Sadly I'm drifting and fading away
Happiness simply ended yesterday's past life makes
no sense not anymore
Is this a nightmare because I can't seem to wake up
I still see you making appearances and giving me
advice
I need to wake up just to see that you're still here and
you didn't really die!!!

<u>He Designed Me</u>

I'm feeling special
I'm feeling creative
I'm feeling motivated
I'm ready to do
What I need to do
To get to my next level
I'm picking up a lot
I'm praying my way through
I don't have to download patience
I'm relieved of the pressure
Of an everyday get me together
Sort of speak my tone
Don't have to be fancy
To address everyday people
In familiar places that I seek
I look in the mirror
I'm staring back and
I'm feeling amazing
He designed me
I grab my phone it's on camera mode
It's selfie time my time to shine
In my own light not even needing a flash
Picture perfect just by being how He designed me

I Don't Know

My passion for you
A gift
I don't know
Your presence
My heart your love
Flowing through secrets
I don't know
No one lives in me
Did you knock
Greeting me
With a hot wet kiss
I don't know
Thoughts crossing
A wondering mind
Chances one may take
I don't know
Torn
To pieces like paper
I don't know
Focus open your eyes
You see that visions of two
Possibles of the possibility
I don't know

<u>My Mood</u>

Is blue and gloomy
Something
Got ahold of me
It won't let me go
Got feelings approaching
Deep down inside me
When the wind blows
My mind shifts
Giving me major
Things to think about
If only I could let go
I would be okay
Sunny days
A smile on my face
Nope
My body
Feeling like a prisoner
In its own skin
Peace
I speak
Please take over me
Silence
My mood incomplete

<u>Nashville</u>

I got a love
For
That place
That I have for no other
High up in the sky
There's a fog
That covers me
I'm at peace
My comfort level
Is high
In dear old Nashville
The sun is hot but
The breeze is cool
My first visit and
I needed a continuation
Two days
Wasn't enough
My heart wasn't ready to leave
My soul stayed
As I got back on that plane
Heading back to a city
Where I no longer connected
Oh my Nashville I will return sooner than later

<u>Long Distance</u>

I hold your hand I feel your beating heart
Through the palm of my hand
Love expands across my mind
Long Distance
You creep into my thoughts I carry you through my
day
You're the comfort I long for
You're the peaceful breeze I feel when the wind
blows
I miss you every waking moment of the day
I picture you sitting in my presence
Looking into my eyes saying words I'll never forget
As happiness fills my soul my heart is open for your
all
Long Distance
Moves me in your direction
You got me taking chances living beyond a dream
You warm me with your beautiful smile
Melting me with your sincere touch
Your sunshine powers up
Tears of a joy that couldn't have come better
The day we met
Your friendship a promise I never want to break
Forever yours no matter how long
Long Distance keeps us apart I keep you in my
heart...

Red Diamond

Demonstrates the heart
Red diamond not silver or blue
I recognize you from far, far away
Even in the distance
My heart beats for you
My love flows for you
I cover myself with your
Precious abundance of peacefulness
The thoughts of just knowing you're there
Waiting to go where no other gem has gone
Red diamond red diamond
You're the jewel that sits in the middle
Not waiting to be discovered
You've been found by me
My eyes designed for your eyes the perfect pair
Red diamond your light so pretty
It shines directly through me
You're perfectly shaped and just the right size
You're special and caring always making things right
Even in the toughest moments you're strong
Even in the weakest moments you're at your best
You're red diamond perfect, a heart designed with a
mighty strength...

Sunshyn Love

<u>My Heart</u>

My heart
Has a problem
Of its own
Can't seem to love
Seems like
There's a block
Of a lock
No key to turn
My heart
Can't connect
Having its own issues
No adjustment
Necessary
Love will find a way
Trusting is an option
One don't
Have to click on
Just go with the flow
Of moving forward
Without regrets
Of what happened
Yesterday will
Greet you tomorrow

February 1990 My Hurt Is Eternal

My precious baby
Raschonda (Tot) got sick
I took her to the doctor
The doctor said
She has pneumonia
Give her liquids
She died
Days later
At the hospital
I will never forget that moment
We were in the room with her
The alarms go off
Doctors and nurses rush in
They told us we had to leave
I'm going around the chair in circles
The nurse tells me to go to waiting room
I'm like huh I'm her mother
The nurse told me I could come back in
After they were done doing what they did
I went to the waiting room praying
My baby was gonna be alright
I'm sitting there the nurse comes in the room
She says I'm sorry
She's gone huh gone gone where
With tears in her eyes she looks at me and says
Your daughter has passed we tried to save her
Tears tears and more tears she said come with me
So you can say your final goodbye huh
I go back to the room and my baby is laying there but
Her eyes are still blinking but her body is still
The nurse is rubbing my back
I'm standing there can't move
The nurse says to me
Your baby is now an angel she's in a better place
I call my mother

Sunshyn Love

The phone is silent and it's like she already knew
What I was calling to say
It was early Sunday morning February 11 1990
My baby was no longer here
I just felt empty unprepared empty
My mother said in a whisper into the phone
Did Raschonda die
Tears cause my baby daughter came into the hospital
alive
Now I had to go home without her forever thank
God for my heart
Cause that's where she resides now in my heart
forever... February 1990

<u>Renovations</u>

I'm tearing down
These walls
That have
Made me feel small
It's time
To clear my mind
A new year
A changing me
It's time
To get my focus
On
I'm doing me
For the better
I'm learning
To understand me
I'm learning to live
Outside the walls
Of my bedroom
I'm opening the door
I'm removing all doubt
Wiping my slate clean
Renovations
Must be made
I'm picking up my feet
So I can see the print
In the sand
I'm reinventing
The way love
Sculptures
My soul
The way my mind
Speaks to my heart
Loving myself
Is an important value
Renovations

Sunshyn Love

Thoughts going down
On paper
Feeling lighter
Relieving stress
Living an understandable
Life
Sometimes facing
Challenging moments
I'll still do my best
When I'm feeling
My worst
Lifting others up
With words of wisdom
Speaking from an extremely
Sincere voice
I'm claiming renovations
Today Tomorrow and Forever
Silence won't cover a mouth
That wants to speak no more
With renovations I'm making valuable moves!

My Mother Named Me Raschon

In Memory of My Mother (Rita Glenda London)

My mother being my first teacher
Taught me to experience growth and
Grow every day and if I should fall back
To be prepared for the ultimate uplifting
IF SOMETHING KNOCKS YOU DOWN
GOD WILL BRING YOU AROUND Amen
She taught me to love everyone
Even if their shoes were bigger
Because it didn't mean
They were better than me
Just meant their feet were larger and
We could all walk the walk
Of going forward and
Moving beyond a shadow of a doubt
My mother was also a creative writer
In her own way sometimes telling a person
Just how she felt most of the time
Leaving them speechless
I kind of have that gentle appeal too
When I write I often enter emotions
Only if what I'm writing is personal and
I need to get my point across in a non-direct way
I can't shake where I came from
Simply because she lives within me
My mother taught me to never live with fear
Always think things through because
You never know who you might need
To get to the next chapter in your life
Or you just never know who may create
The next story of your life you must live and learn
The value of your journey your truth on the positive
side
A little bit of knowledge from living in a caring

Sunshyn Love

environment:
My mother had a house full of plants and
As a little girl I often wondered
Why she had so many of them and
Why she would talk to them
When she watered them
As growth took me through the years
I figured it out it's because she nurtured them
Just like she nurtured her daughters and she held
nothing back
Not even when it came to her calling us by
Our whole name her voice got us to moving fast
Remember life has all kinds of directions choose your
route carefully
Never give up on your journey if you should run into
a stop sign
Imagine going nowhere when the light turns green
keep your focus
Moving forward on a mission with a cause the
experience of being named Raschon!

Don't Sugar Coat Hurt

People judge you
Never
Knowing
The truth
Even if stories
Are
Three-sided
You know
What you been
Through
Behind
Closed doors
Everything
Wasn't good
The grass
Was never too green
On the other side
Of the fence
Creating problems
Families
Taking sides
Showing
A real darkness
When
The other day
There was no light
The battle
Of empty thoughts
Running
Through your head
Cause
This negro
Then put his hands
On you
In the worst way

Sunshyn Love

When it was just
You two
Behind the closed door
No sympathy
Needed
Just
Clear words
That
Greets the common
Heart
Falling at the seams
Of an
Unstitched pattern
All it takes is
One string to pull it all apart
If you can help one person
Help yourself
Get out of that situation
Live
Love don't make
You suffer from hurt and pain
No matter
What the people say
Looking through the window
The journey you walk
Will always be your story
Tell it to help others
Going through what you been through
Completion is what helps you grow
Worded correctly
You can't tell me about my struggle
Until you've walked in my shoes
Knock on my door
There's more to the story
Than what you been told
Love yourself more than abuse

<u>One Line Drama</u>

No two minds think the same
But
You read me like a magical book
Knowing my thoughts before I think
If loving you is wrong
I really don't want to be right
So when
I touch you
In the night we'll both be right
There will be
All smiles and no frowns
On your inspired face
As you gift me with encouragement
Lifting my mind while our spirits fly
If loving you is wrong
I want to be your midnight light
That you follow when things in
Your life have you feeling down
Trusting and believing how love is right
If loving you is wrong
Let's look
Out the window and count millions of stars together
Making wishes of a lifetime keeping us both focused
100%.

<u>After the Conversation</u>

I
Just wanted to
Go home and
Sleep so
I could dream
A tiredness
Took over
My body
Laying down
Is what
I needed to do
Feelings caught
Me slipping
Now I'm
Feeling
A type of way
I'm praying for the best
I just don't want to feel
My worst
When the time comes
I know
With wings
We must fly and
Decisions we must make
Sometimes right
Seems to make us
Go left but
We must pray for direction
It's like losing
A friend and
Regaining
A family member
From long ago
Feeling blessed
From the presence

Of being in my life
I can't let go
My heart keeps telling me
This is deeper than
Building a bridge and
Taking a walk to
Release feelings
As
Mountains and hills
Will soon divide us
I'm realizing
The travel of going on is real
I'm at a standstill
After the conversation
Piles of words
No voice
Silence treads lightly
Through a tunnel
Of a mind with
Tears in the eyes
Letting them go
Relieves
How one is feeling
Sometimes
You have to speak up
Except the words won't
Come out right
Leaving a soul speechless
Emptiness finds
A strong bond
That can't be broken
Yet
There's no soothing
Emotions are a wreck
Love lifted
Started from the ground
Up

Sunshyn Love

Seeds were planted
This just didn't
Happen overnight
It was a process
That needed to grow
Through all seasons
Falling into place
Never thought
After The Conversation
I'd be up
Trying to figure out
Where to go from here
Trusting and relaxing
A comfortable feeling
Backing off seems to be
What's happening
For just a moment
A voice with no message
Can't be heard
Actions behind the scenes
This is life not a play
After The Conversation!

<u>When My Best Depended On You</u>

As life would have it I found myself needing help
So as I was on my way to the clinic for my
appointment
I prayed that I would receive some kind of help
I pulled into the parking lot still praying and
Listening to gospel music my world had been turned
upside down
I didn't know you would be my help Dr. even though
Others had told me I needed counseling and after
what
Had happened I believed so too just didn't know who
Or where I would go to receive help I had no options
God put you in my life I believe because
A pain had formed in a special place in my body
My heart I looked to you to undo my hurt
As talking things out with you seemed to help clear
my thoughts
When my best depended on you I'm grateful you
were there
So glad that God placed you in my life
At that moment and time a welcomed blessing
You are truly someone easy to talk to
Listening to me with patience as sometimes I really
didn't know
How to express exactly how I was feeling you simply
gave me the floor
I talked you listened then you talked never
condemning my feelings
Simply trying to help ease my situation you opened a
door for me
That has always been kept closed and I thank you
from the bottom of my heart
A difference is definitely being made, I'm not there
yet but a healing has begun!

<u>Gone But Never Forgotten</u>

In my own world
I just need
To hear your words of wisdom
I wait for your morning call
I say ring phone ring
The phone is silent
As I realize my phone
Will never ring
With your number again
Tears
Start to roll down my face
As realizing me talking to you
I can't do anymore
As I listen to my voicemail
Hearing you say
Call me back Shon
I start to dial your number
Then I realize
I now have to call you up
On your special phone
Cause now
You have a new home
Heaven!!!! I never knew my first poem in print would
be your obituary!!!!!

Betrayed

I.

Happy, happy
Joyful, joyful
To the tears you caused
Never thinking
Never minding me
Laughter used to fill the air
Now tears of sadness cover a face
At first I couldn't understand
How one could
Betray
My soul says fix it
My spirit says leave it alone
My heart says he never loved you anyway
So let it go
The pain will ease
Life without him
A gift without sin
Betrayed

II.

Cheers of wisdom used to greet me
Got a heart feeling sad
As I lay in the bed
Like the tree's slow sway of
An unknown journey
With an unwinding breeze on a cold brutal night
Stars shine but
The truth to the light is dim
Life not the expected but the unexpected
Betrayed
You had me but you don't got me
I got out that web
Thought you had me but you don't got me
I got out that web

Sunshyn Love

Thought you had me trapped
I'm a fighter
Just not fighting for you
I'm a lover
Just not loving you
Anymore
A miracle happened I had a dream
I seen several lights
Red light after red light now
I give you the green light
Betrayed no more!!!!!

Life on the Other Side of the Mountain

My heart no longer lives in the city where I reside
Changes I need to make are at a standstill
Fear has rushed me head-on
I really don't know what to do
My spirit tells me go, go, go but
Family and friends won't understand
The move I need to make
Is with good faith and judgment
Life on the other side of the mountain
Awaits me my soul is slowly drifting away
Flowing to a new destination I'm ready for change
As only I know decisions, decisions I must make
What's left here for me?
Every part of me has left and went south for a new
beginning
Life on the other side of the mountain
Where my destiny awaits me
A new life, a new home and a new me
Change is coming I spread my arms
As I choose to cross over the rainbow
Bypassing the stars and the moon deeply inside I
must go
It's all about starting fresh and new
Happy moments will arise I won't forget where I
came from
Only concentrating on my new lease on life
So I stand proudly as I choose to live
Life on the other side of the mountain!!!

<u>Cowgirl</u>

I want to be a cowgirl
I want to feel free
I want to seek a vision
I never seen before
Time to get right
Time for change
Time to let my thoughts flow
I'm going to get a horse
I'm going to travel the countryside
A happiness shows on my face
I will think about my life
I will make my path
I will climb mountains
Reach victories and clear my mind
A house is not a home
If you got everything and you still feel alone
I got to start somewhere
As I know it simply begins with me
The emptiness that fills my insides
Will no longer exist
I won't worry about what others have to say
My heart says go
I'm on my way to a new beginning
I must push on past these bitter thoughts holding me
back
My journey awaits me I'm bout to become a
Cowgirl
It's my life I got to live it
I must go on I will return
With a great motivation
My mission will be complete
As I pack my patience
I promise to return with peace
I got my boots, jeans and cowgirl hat
I'm ready

I'm about to saddle up and get gone
A pretty horse I will ride
As my hair blows free
Clearing my mind I deserve this
As the wind whisks my thoughts away
I will take time for me
The horse will do the walking
As I travel through the woods
Picking wildflowers oh the colors will be pretty
What a fun experience this is going to be
I'm leaving city life behind
If only for a day it's going to be the best day
Nothing will matter just me having fun
On the countryside playing in the hay
A dream will be fulfilled a cowgirl is in me!!!

<u>I Got a Smile on My Face</u>

I got a smile on my face
I'm happy on the inside
No matter what people say
They can't take my joy away
Having a fabulous day
Happy on the inside
I got love in my heart and
That's where it starts
I'm happy on the inside
Believing in me
Why can't you see?
I got a smile on my face
I'm happy on the inside
I got a pep in my step
I'm headed in the right direction
As joy comes in the morning
Brightly the sun will come out shining
Faith is what keeps me going
Over above and beyond
Feeling great feeling great
Oh
I got a smile on my face
I'm happy on the inside!!!

Past Few Months

These past few months
We have come together
We fussed but we made things happen
Haven't seen this much family
Since a funeral
Cousins dropping in to see how
Everything's going
What an amazing setup
Kids working our nerves until we fed them
Wishing well we jamming to the beat
Makes you want to get up doing your own dance
I even added me a verse had me feeling like singing
Just to say it wasn't rehearsal
If Angie wasn't fussing and hollering clean my floor
and
Shut the front door then back to rehearsal we go
Movements of the stomping of feet as we tried to
figure out the beat
Soon as we got it here comes her landlord saying we
shaking his house and
He's used to it being quiet as a mouse but all in all
Family time is what this was all about enjoying seeing
everybody
It was about commitment Angie, Mila, Brandy, Ciera,
Andrea, Chantinye, Deshanta
Sometimes Danielle lending a hand
We pulled it off even when it looked bleak and we
threw our hands up saying
Forget it nobody got time for this trying to rehearse
with these hard-headed kids!!!

Sunshyn Love

<u>Having a Woman Power</u>

It allows us so much strength
Becoming a woman
Was no overnight thing
It takes time and patience
To reach your destination
It's not on your mark
Get set go you're a woman
No
That's not how it happens
You have to grow
Become experienced
Talk to others
Who's been where you're trying to go
Believe this nobody's road was easy
There's always been stumbles
Dead-ends and wake-up calls
The things I know now
I didn't know when I was 20 or even 30
I had to look back on my life
Cut some rope in order to move on
The things that used to blindfold me
I see right through the foolishness
Woman Power Activated

<u>Cold Shoulder</u>

I got you the perfect gift hope you like it
Not packaged because I needed you to feel it
A cold-shoulder awwww glad you like it
It's being given to you out of loyalty and respect
It's by no chance an accident or a waste of time
When the shoulder was nice and warm for you
That was too much tempting and loving going on
So you took it for granted left the shoulder hanging
Not just once but a bunch of times
You can't borrow somebody's time like it's free
Time is priceless and never given away
Just a thought: Have you ever felt pained and
Couldn't relax your mind anxiety taking over your
thoughts
Even when the truth was right there in your face
So you had to take a minute look in the mirror
Asking yourself did I just get cold-shouldered simply
The person staring back at you got the yes look the
same as you do
So putting up a guard is necessary and the cold-
shoulder a must
First you got to do unto her as you would want her to
do unto you
So feel the breeze and enjoy it like being in the
standing-room-only with no invitation
Being left out in the cold don't feel so good now does
it
So before you think you're being funny and think
you're running game
Lay on this cold-shoulder and revolve on that ice
pack, who got the cold-shoulder now?

<u>Unauthorized</u>

These feelings that I'm feeling
Unauthorized
The love that flows
Through my warrantied soul
Unauthorized
The treasures that fill my chest
Unauthorized
The words that keep changing my mind
Unauthorized
The looks that leave me feeling incomplete
Unauthorized
The following of my footprints
As I no longer know where I'm going
Unauthorized
The sadness that fills my heart with grief
Unauthorized
A friendship that doesn't seem to be there
No matter how much I try
Unauthorized
The tears that swell my eyes
As too much is going on leaving me troubled
Unauthorized
Emails and messages sent but left unopened,
unauthorized...

Jesus Is My Keeper

Jesus is my keeper
He gave me a smile on a cloudy day
Jesus is my keeper
He lifted me up
When I had no way of getting up
Jesus is my keeper
Did you know
He washed all my sins away
Jesus is my keeper
Jesus is my keeper
He watched me sleep
Then woke me up to see another day
Jesus is my keeper
He put me through tests
I have a testimony
Jesus is my keeper
While I was on my journey
Passing through the storm
He was there waiting on me
Jesus like no other
Jesus is my keeper
Jesus is my keeper
I'm not afraid to let
Anyone know
Jesus is my keeper
He's my best friend
Never telling
My secrets and
He makes a way
Out of no way
Jesus is my keeper
He's for me
When others are against me
Jesus is my keeper
O O O O O YES

Sunshyn Love

Jesus is my keeper
I accepted Him
Back in the day
He never ever left me
Always been
By my side and
In my heart
I'm a
Jesus believer
A Jesus believer
Simply
Jesus Is My Keeper...
Jesus Is My Keeper
He picked me up
Turned me around
When I was heading
The wrong way
Jesus is my keeper
When sickness
Covered my body
He healed me
My sickness
Washed away
Jesus is my keeper
Jesus is my keeper
When things started happening
I didn't understand why
Jesus stepped in
Jesus is my keeper
Jesus is my keeper
When bills were due and
My money was short
I didn't worry
I trusted in Jesus, I trusted in Jesus
He made everything alright
Jesus is my keeper, Jesus is my keeper!!!

<u>By Faith</u>

My character, My body
My soul, My strength
My spirit
An angel above me
Sent from Heaven from the beautiful skies
To the sun shining
To the wet feeling of raindrops getting all of my
attention
As my inspiration inspires me
My motivation sets a pace
Of walking the ground
I once stood on
My footprints engraved
Letting me know
To never forget where I came from and
How I got to my destination
Well it was by the Grace of God
He delivered me strength
When I was weak
He picked me up when I was down
He created a smile when I could only produce a
frown
He kept me He guided me He protected me
In the midst of everything including the storms
That came my way my journey has just begun...

<u>World</u>

Lost in a world
That owes
Me nothing
I got to get up
Make things happen
Doing
What lifts me up
Keeps me calm
Remembering
Happiness lights
My world
Set no limits
Go above and beyond
I believe in me
Traditionally
I always wanted to be a
WRITER
I know this now that
Even if my thinking skills
Are off I got to
RELAX
Stay patient and everything
Will flow when it's time
EVEN
In my finest moments
I have to always give myself
TIME
To get my thoughts together
I may have to write them down
Then give myself a break
Reread and edit
If necessary
No writing skills are basic
Just write what you feel
Judge not

What I write simply
It doesn't have to make sense
Because
Feelings are feelings
Coming from the inside
SOMETIMES
Never making any sense at all
LOVING
To be an entertainer
Through the joys of writing
Just know putting the wrong words
Can be like entertainment
To the reader leaving them to
Their own imagination
In my world
I created my own type of work
My way my thoughts
I put myself in imaginary positions
Focusing on the positive side of things
For the most part keep in mind
Me the writer is human just like you
In general my favorite work is when
I let my wandering mind take over
Inviting my alter ego in I call her
Sunshyn Love
She's very secure In Her Own Thoughts
She
Secretly talks Raschon into writing
A lot of difficult things she wouldn't
Ordinarily write for the utmost
She's gifted and talented her mind flows free
With peace and passion
Her work with a little play every now and again
Trust I love writing it's my heart of expressions
When my words won't come out my mouth
I put them in writing so everyone can see I can speak
both ways!

<u>My Friend</u>

Comes with hands
To hold mine
When I'm in need of comfort
My friend
Comes with eyes
To see me
When I'm feeling down
My friend
Comes with ears
To listen to me
When I need to vent
My friend
Comes with a mouth
To speak soft words
When I'm feeling hurt
My friend
Comes with no clock
Giving me
All the needed time
I need to speak
My friend hears my thoughts thinks my thoughts
Simply we're connected through our heavenly spirits!

<u>Read My Lips</u>

If loving you is wrong
I know this is no mistake
I want to love you with all my heart
I really
Want to be right so when
I touch you in the night
I'll see all smiles on your charming face
Living life without you would be all wrong
If loving you relieves stress
I'll rather have peace with you
A secret it wouldn't be
Coming from me to you
If letting the whole world know
What's going through me for you
Is my love designed wholeheartedly
For you
I'll stand on the mountain top
Opening my mouth screaming
So the world would know
I'll do just that
Read my lips
Every day I whisper my love for you
These words live in me undressing all my thoughts

I Can't Fight This Battle (Tell Your Story Help Somebody)

Why can't I fight this battle I keep trying to let it go
but
It keeps sneaking back up on me even when I sleep
He put his hands on me in the wrong way
I used to be afraid to talk about it for fear of what
others would say
Today it's time to clean out my closet and let it go
Abused Physical and Mental When I Was Married so
I say
I won't let you hurt me again through your words or
physical abuse
I prayed about it in the past the devil got in my way
because
I kept accepting your apology but today I'm in
control no more sorry
To My Abuser: You called me names that weren't fit
for a sheep
I almost started believing you when you said no one
else wanted me
Except you the lies you tell you only wanted me to be
your punching bag
Today I live without your fear I challenged myself to
move on
I had a lot of work to do on my end I suffered a lot
of damage
You tried to mold me into what you wanted me to be
a weak little girl
I have grown so much since then I recognize bull
crap before it gets to me
I had to cross a couple of paths I knew I had to hold
on and help was on the way
I had to take off the shackles and release and let it go
I didn't forget I let it go

I had to surrender my soul I thought my scars would
last forever just the ugly thoughts
When you only seen the worst in me God's
unchanging hands
He saw the best no matter what you said or did to me
the powers that be
This sister right here stayed prayed up even though
my self-esteem was so low
I still had to struggle with an undesired battle waking
up scared and unsettled
Why Can't I Fight This Battle
I was walking around with my head down I never
wanted to look up or smile
People used to ask me is it that bad I would respond
if only you knew if only you knew
I lived it my life I learned from it my story every time
I mean every time
He hit me hours later he said he loved me and said
how sorry he was
At that time I didn't know love wasn't supposed to
hurt
All the nights I stayed up fearing from not knowing if
this was my last day of life
I thank God for making me stronger and grateful for
all the people who had my back
When I needed them the most rather it was just talk
or just lending me their ear
These words right here is what got me to see the light,
which made sense
If you not gone change your situation then why keep
talking about it
Do something about it do something about it do
something about it
Leave and don't look back have no regrets when you
pack up your stuff
Walk out that door with your head high remember
none of the abuse is your fault

Sunshyn Love

You can make it on your own just pray and keep
praying don't worry about how
You're going to make it this battle is not yours God
got your back just goooooooo
With your life please you have to trust your own
instincts move on with your dignity
Of course it's going to be scary and doubts will fill
your mind
You have to remember you are not a punching bag
you're human and love don't hurt
Love yourself enough to leave and after you get
yourself together
Take time to breathe take time to learn you
It's going to be ok it really is
Jesus will make a way believe that live your life
without physical and mental abuse
Changes have to be made so you can move forward
you must like and love you
No strings attached cut the strings until you feel
better let go of the anger feel better!!!

<u>Digging Deep</u>

Can't sleep Can't eat Can't figure me out so I got to
dig deep
I reach in my pocket nothing's there I touch my heart
I feel a little beat
I can't hide this no more this pain is taking me over
I'm happy one minute crying the next
My right hand can't seem to hold on my left hand got
to hold all the weight
I have an ache no medicine can control it as it comes
and goes from
The fear of being all alone got me digging deep I put
my shoes on but
The walk of life is useless I ask myself over and over
again why did you have to go
Leaving me here as I was on a deserted island
No answers no answers no answers I was unprepared
for that night
Didn't even receive a signal no light came on
You always said you got me just lift your head a smile
would connect me to look but
Not anymore sadness wakes me up in the middle of
the night
As a single whisper I hear is that you telling me good
night
Digging deep I'm traveling a road and going nowhere
I count the stars I often see one twinkle right beneath
the moon
A light I see shines brightly I have to close my eyes
and
Begin to dream about the good times and bad ones
too
Then I feel stronger because now you're my wind
beneath my wings
I keep hearing your voice you're telling me you lived
your life

Sunshyn Love

I wake up and begin to pray because that boy took
your life
You had just made it up the ladder a higher position
bigger pay
The day you told me I was happy for you because the
battle of surviving
Day to day was now over and you could feel proudly
again of a win-win!!!

<u>On The Receiving End</u>

I'm learning as I live
Each day with a vision
I own what I'm feeling
No words can describe
How I'm feeling
When a difference matters
The ride of a blessing
Comes in all
Sizes, colors and ages
Near or far
Distance just doesn't matter
When you're delivered and
The only thing you can do
Is fly high and
Spread the mighty wings
Of determination
When you're on the receiving end
Balancing love and like
Actions showed speak louder
Than some of
The words coming from the lips
A voice so dear inside you
Knows what's traveling through the mind always

<u>Special Feelings</u>

As beautiful
As life is
We'll all like to stay here
On Earth forever
Beautiful is
The flowers
The trees
Maybe just to feel the breeze
The calming of the wind
On a silent night
The moon lighting up the sky
With the stars shining through
While we wish upon a dream
Life's happiest moments
Remain with us forever
Building up hopes frozen in time
Memories we'll love to share
Snapshots in a picture album
The heavens above blue skies
Imagine the rainbow appearing
High up above magically showering
Your joy lifting temptations of faith
Smiley faces no reason for a frown
You walk
Your path guided from high up
You can't go wrong
With Jesus by your side
The wonderful world of music
There's a song
Playing in your head
I see you
Stepping never missing a beat
You're happy couldn't imagine you sad
Just beautiful in and out
Your voice the words you speak

Never bringing anyone down
Living for a powerful uplifting
You can do it
I know you can just believe
In yourself
In the power of being a better you
Forever
Life gets no better than that
Remember
Recycle your love
Everlasting
Soul touching good feeling everyday
Sharing make a person's day beautiful

www.ingramcontent.com/pod-product-compliance
Lightning Source LLC
LaVergne TN
LVHW051154080426
835508LV00021B/2631